I0475162

Hook Yourself up:
Pricing Crochet For Profit

Sedruola N. Maruska

ISBN: 978-1-365-37854-6

Introduction

"Oh wow, that's so beautiful, will you make me one?" That question used to stop me dead in my tracks when I first started to crochet. I wasn't sure what to say. Most times I picked a random number that felt comfortable for me or that was just enough to cover my costs.

When I decided to start a business I did the same thing. That was a mistake. I followed the formula that was to triple my supplies, but found that sometimes it fell very short of what I really needed to make a profit. Things began to turn around when I realized that I needed to consider much more than just supplies in my pricing.

This book is to help you get to that conclusion faster than I did. Of all the questions I get, by far, "*how much should I charge for my crochet work?*" is number one. The question about pricing crochet is both objective and subjective. Some of what you'll do in crochet is not in your control to price, while others depend completely on your business.

Just like all businesses, the pricing on your crochet items and skills are at your discretion. It's the main reason the time and research you put into figuring out your target audience and what it will bear will help dictate your pricing. So it's a sliding scale depending on your audience and business.

This book gives you information and calculations that will help set prices for your pieces. It also gives you information to make an educated decision on whether other opportunities, within the arena of crochet, are worth your time when presented with offers. We'll talk about pricing completed pieces, all the way to speaking engagements.

Making money with your crochet skills is exciting. I've tried to cover the different ways you can make money with crochet and be fairly compensated for your skills and time. You have a skill and you've decided to make it work for you. Congratulations! Once you know your crochet business/hobby goals, you'll have the foundation for confidence in your pricing and delivering to the marketplace.

I'm so excited to write this book for you. So grab your pen, paper and calculator and let's get on the road to developing a pricing strategy that works for you no matter what area you've decided to focus on in your crochet business!

Chapter 1
Marketing Basics

Let's start off easy with marketing basics. If you don't know marketing basics, you won't know how to price. Pricing is all about your business needs meeting your target audience needs.

Let's take a blow pop for example. A blow pop costs $.25. The target audience is non-working, young and loves candy! They have no concept of money; they just know they want the pop and they can probably find $.25 around their house or in their piggy bank. The makers of the blow pop have made the packaging colorful and fun to attract their target audience's attention. They have also priced the candy well within range.

If the makers of the Blow Pop didn't know their target audience, and only considered everything that surrounds the making of one pop so that the pricing might have ended up somewhere around $1.50 they might not be in business today.

That's why you need to know a bit of marketing basics to begin to talk about price.

Product / Service

What are you selling? Because this book is specifically for crochet artists, I'm going to assume it's something associated with crochet.What is it specifically that you're selling? Are you selling one-of-a-kind elaborate headpieces? Or, do you specialize in fast, easy hats & scarves? Do you sell housewares or intricate afghans?

The reason I ask is if you don't know your product, how can you effectively sell it? To sell an afghan that takes hours of your time at the flea market for less than the cost of materials is a sure way to go out of business within weeks.

If crochet is a hobby, and you don't mind financing it with your family income, by all means, sell it for whatever price you feel comfortable. If what you want is for your crochet business to grow and thrive, then keep reading because we're getting through the first steps to help you get to the pricing.

Crochet allows you to make money in many ways. Here are just a few:

- Selling completed pieces
- Selling patterns
- Publishing articles / patterns
- Teaching
- Public Speaking
- Pattern Testing
- Contract Crocheting

How to price for each of these areas will be covered in this book to help your crochet business grow.

Having a clear understanding of what you plan to offer the marketplace is key in helping you decide who your audience is, where to find them, and what they'll pay.

Start with what you want to sell and keep moving.

Target Audience

The Blow Pop analogy is easy, so let's keep going with it.

The makers of the Blow Pop probably sat down at the beginning of development and decided who they would be selling to. That's what you need to do. They will be your target audience.

Can we all eat Blow Pops? Yes. Can we all afford Blow Pops? Yes. Do we all eat Blow Pops? Maybe.

I'll venture to say it's possible that we've eaten a Blow Pop while considered outside of the target audience.

When the executives were in that room they probably knew everyone could enjoy a Blow Pop, but they needed to make a decision about who exactly they wanted to target. That's what you need to do.

Sit down with a pad and paper and figure out who you want to target to purchase your items. When I say who, I mean create a picture of what they look like, what they want and need and where you can find them. Without this step, considering pricing is useless.

When you take time to answer the question "Who is my target audience?" you'll find it easier to figure out other aspects of your marketing. If you do the hard work first, it will point you squarely in the direction you need to go to calculate your item pricing.

Branding

I've never seen a Blow Pop in brown packaging with gold letters, have you? I'm going to go out on a limb to say it's because their audience would completely ignore that packaging.

I have seen brown and gold packaging on chocolates meant for a much more sophisticated audience. Packaging is part of the Blow Pop brand. Light, colorful, and easy to spot is directly associated with the target audience selected for Blow Pops. The executives know their audience is drawn to fun and happy colors, so they've wrapped their pops in fun and happy packaging with rainbows of neon colors and polka dots!

When it comes to your business and knowing your target audience, how are you branding yourself? Is your branding too sophisticated for the audience you've picked or too simple? Will your branding attract your audience, turn them away or just be invisible to them? Because you know your target audience, you'll get into their heads and decide what branding will work best.

Now, let's pause here and say that a lot of what you do depends on your needs and wants. What your company image (aka. Branding) looks like is personal. You're also responsible for picking the audience you'll work with, so everything should be interesting to both you and your audience.

Branding your business includes things like your logo, your colors, your wording, your packaging and your set-up. Keeping everything consistent helps create your brand and your message to your target audience. I could write a separate book on branding, so I'll stop here because I think you get the idea. The bottom line is this, the branding you do plays a part in your pricing because of your audience.

Selling Venue

I don't think Versace will sell at Target. Why? Well, I'm pretty sure they know most Target shoppers are not going to consider paying their prices. Why, then, do I see fiber artists trying so hard to sell their creations at venues that won't understand their value?

Where you sell, again, depends on the people you want to reach and the price you want for your pieces. If you want to do craft shows, you need to know and understand the audience that will be there so you'll know which of your pieces will sell best at that show to the audience you will expect to find there. There's nothing wrong with having multiple strategies to reach different audiences but you need to know which audience you're presenting to and what their needs are.

Where can you sell crochet pieces? Here are some possibilities:

- Flea markets
- Free craft fairs
- Juried craft fairs
- Farmers markets
- Consignment shops
- Boutiques
- Online store (3rd party host)
- Online store (self-hosted)
- Online auction site
- Local Yarn Shop
- Wholesale

Whichever of these venues you select depends on what you've learned about your target audience. The venue will also play a large part in what you can charge for your work. There are different audiences for each of these venues. Some overlap, but that's what you need to discover in your research and use to make the best decision for sale venue as possible.

Budget

The last area is budget. Marketing your inventory is an ongoing effort that will be an investment. Figuring out what that investment is ahead of time will help you figure out where and how to market your business. There are endless ways to market your business, ranging from free to thousands of dollars. Because you'll already know your target audience, you'll know where to find them and how to reach them. Use your budget in those areas.

I see statements all the time that say, "you need to spend at least $____ to reach your audience." The problem with that statement is that they probably haven't read your marketing plan, so they really can't talk to your situation.

Whatever your budget, spend it wisely. If you have the opportunity to showcase your items at the local craft fair, but you know that only a small percentage of your audience will be there, figure out for yourself if the cost is worth your time. Your marketing budget is the lifeblood of your business. Guard it well.

Chapter 2
Pricing & Selling Completed Pieces

Now we get into the fun stuff!

By now you realize that pricing can't be done in a vacuum or on a whim. Pricing is done with purpose. You now also know that your prices are wrong. Not really, but you're probably re-evaluating the pricing strategy you've been using and how it's keeping you from your goal. Pricing too high or too low can both keep you from your goal and from your target audience. Pricing just right will let you meet your expenses and give you a profit. Let's start!

This book will give you ideas on how to price your pieces depending on where you sell and your goal. Remember, you are the only one who can know if a pricing strategy is going to work for you and your target audience.

If a formula isn't right for you, adjust it to your needs. Guidelines are not rules; they are starting points, so that's what these are. The guidelines in this book will help you make great choices when it comes to your crochet business.

Production Costs

To figure out a fair market value on anything you're selling, you need to know what your costs are to create that piece. Once you know your basic production costs, you can then figure out pricing for venues.

How do you figure out your production costs? Let's start with finding our total costs on a monthly basis. Let's say we make 10 scarves in a month. Keeping that in mind, let's do some math calculations. Ugh, math, I know, but if you're a crocheter, you can't get away from math because it's all over every piece you create. So, let's try to embrace the math thing and use it to figure out the best pricing for all the lovely work you do.

To figure out the production cost for those scarves we need to:

Calculate Total Fixed costs for the month – Total Fixed Costs are expenses you have on a regular basis every month. They don't change no matter how many scarves you sell. (e.g. Website, rent, subscription fees, service fees, marketing budget, etc.)

Calculate Total Variable costs for the month – Total Variable Costs are expenses directly related to the creation and sale of the scarves. (e.g. cost of materials, shipping cost, listing or selling fees, number of hours to produce, etc.)

Your cost per scarf will then be calculated like this:

Keep in mind this is not your retail price; this number is just what it will cost you to create each scarf per month. So, if we want to work in fantasy numbers, the calculation will be:

($83 + $372 / 10 scarves = $45.50 cost per scarf)

The number you get is the starting point for all your pricing going forward. Remember, the cost per scarf may change depending on the changes in your variable costs related to your monthly business volume, but for this example we'll keep the costs steady.

Wholesale Pricing

Starting with wholesale pricing is strategic. If and/or when a store buyer contacts you to buy your pieces to sell in their store, you need to have a pricing sheet that will let you still make a profit on your pieces. If you start with a retail price, without having thought of a wholesale strategy, you'll lose money by selling to that retail buyer. Or worst, they may not be interested because their profit margin will be too low. So, let's take our Cost Per Unit, or Production Cost, that we found in the last section and figure out our wholesale price.

Wholesale price is the price you offer to retailers to purchase your items and "retail" in their shop. For you to make sure that both you and the retailer are making enough of a profit margin on each item, it's important that you figure out your wholesale cost. A formula for that is:

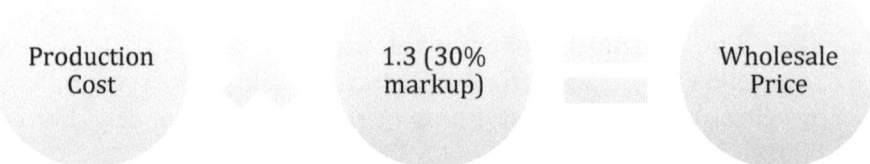

| Production Cost | 1.3 (30% markup) | Wholesale Price |

So if we consider the wholesale price on our scarves it would look like this:

$45.50 x 1.3 (30% markup) = $59.15 Wholesale

This pricing will give you a cushion of about $13.65, so you make money when wholesaling your pieces. You'll also give the retailer a Suggested Retail Price that they may or may not honor, but at least you've made a good sale for your business.

Retail Pricing

Retail pricing is usually the place most crochet business owners begin. As you can see, it's not the best starting point. There is an old understanding that if you start high, it's easier to lower your price, but if you start low, it's difficult to raise your price. When starting with the retail price in mind first, you're more likely to start too low and find it uncomfortable to raise the price when you figure out your costs and what goes into your craft business.

Let's work on a few scenarios that will help us figure out the best retail pricing for our scarves.

Suggested Retail Price

If you've sold your items to a retailer at wholesale, it's a good idea to give them a Suggested Retail Price so they can see what their possible margin can be on the sale of your pieces. Whether they use that price or not is not up to you, since you've already sold your pieces to them. Here's a formula to help you figure out a suggested retail price:

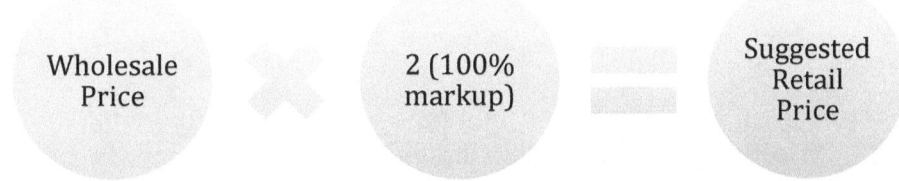

Wholesale Price × 2 (100% markup) = Suggested Retail Price

So if we consider the suggested retail price on our scarves, it would look like this:

$59.15 x 2 = $118.30 SRP per scarf

Remember, this is just a suggestion to the retailer, but it gives you a good margin to work with when figuring out your personal retail price.

Retail Price

You probably bought this book because you sell items on the market. I hope that so far you've found value in what you've learned. Now you're ready to consider your pricing. You're selling crochet to make a profit, but you also want to make sure to price for the market and for your target audience.

Continuing with our scarf project, there are a few ways to consider your retail price, and they all come from the wholesale price. Why? The wholesale price gives you the chance to make a profit. There will be times when you want to use your production cost as a starting point but they are very few.

Remember, if you use the production cost as the basis for your retail price, your profit margin will be lower.

Selling Online/Personal Boutique

If you're selling in your own shop online or in the real world, it's a good idea to use one of the following formulas to figure out your price:

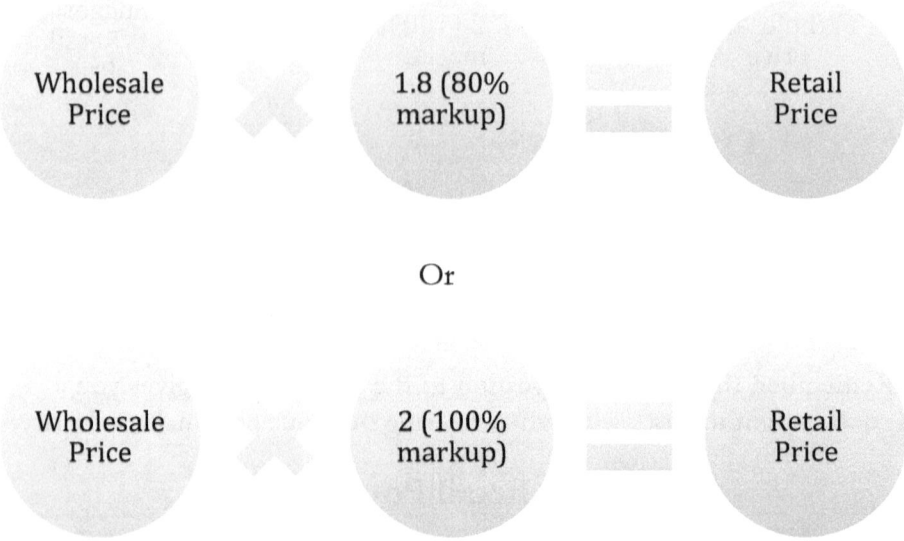

Or

Using our scarf scenario:

$59.15 x 1.8 = $106.47 per scarf

$59.15 x 2 - $118.30 per scarf

Either price is fine because they're still within the profit margin and not undercutting your wholesale buyers. Clearly one has a higher profit margin than the other. It's a matter of choice and judgment which price you choose.

Selling at a Craft Show

Selling at a craft show has a few variables that I'd like to point out. I won't change the numbers we've been working with. If you sell at a craft show you'll have the added cost of paying for the space, travel, and set-up items. Make sure to keep that in mind as an added variable cost in the months you do shows.

In my experience, depending on the show, most craft show buyers are looking for something "different," and if it isn't different, they're looking for a "bargain." That's okay, as long as you know that going in and you've prepared for it.

To price for a show, you can use the same retail pricing you have calculated for your shop, but if you think the show will be one where a lower price is more appropriate, here are some options:

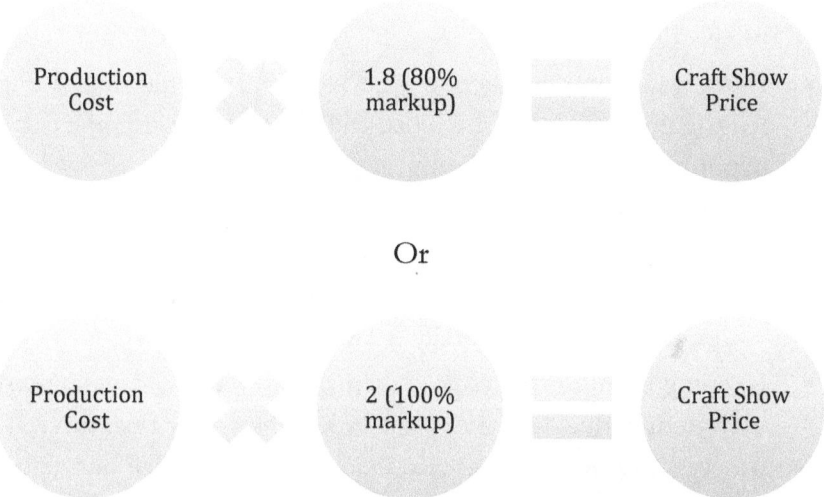

Or

Using our scarf scenario:

$$\$45.50 \times 1.8 = \$81.90 \text{ per scarf}$$

$$\$45.50 \times 2 = \$91.00 \text{ per scarf}$$

This is the ONLY time I will suggest using the production cost as the basis vs. using the wholesale cost and ONLY if you feel your prices need to be lowered. Otherwise, always use your wholesale price as the basis. Also, I'd like for you to remember that some people at the craft show may "haggle" on price, so consider that when figuring out your price per piece for the show.

Flea Market Pricing

Selling at the flea market, if you've decided that's where your target audience will be, can work out well for you. When pricing your pieces for the flea market, remember that part of the fun is price haggling, so make sure you price accordingly. Some general guidelines for pricing for the flea market include:

- Mark the price on each item so the buyer is clear. Don't keep a pricelist in your head.
- Use whole numbers such as $5, $10, $15, etc. That makes it easy for the buyer to leave the loose change in their car and carry only paper bills.
- Use numbers that seem lower but are close enough to the price you really want. If you'd like to sell an item for $100, drop the price to $95, making is easier for your buyer to look at the item without walls being mentally drawn.
- Keeping in mind that your audience may want to haggle; mark each item with a "haggle" price rather than your final price. That way you can negotiate a price below the listed price but higher than your bottom price.

Now that we've gotten that down, let's use some formulas to make it easier. Here are some ideas for pricing you may want to consider:

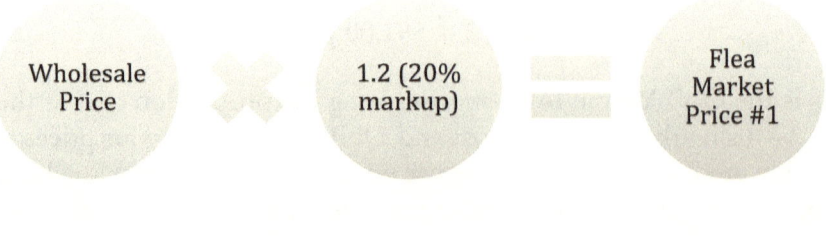

Or

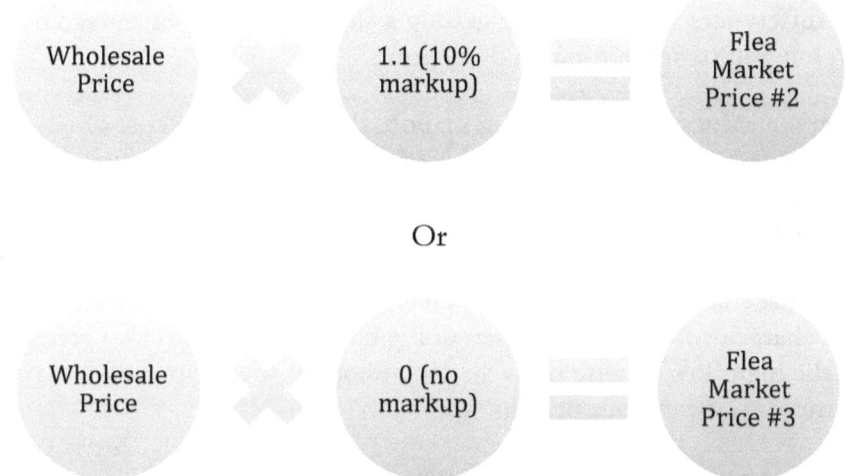

Or

Using our scarf scenario:

$$\$59.15 \times 1.2 = \$70.98 \text{ (flea mkt price of \$70)}$$

$$\$59.15 \times 1.1 = \$65.07 \text{ (flea mkt price of \$65)}$$

$$\$59.15 \text{ (30\% markup built in)}$$

Remember your wholesale price already has a profit margin of 30%, so you won't lose by using that number. But, if you go any lower than the wholesale price, you will cut into your profit and be moving down to "cost."

Selling on Consignment

Sometimes a shop wants to test pieces in their store and/or they don't want to take the full cost of carrying your pieces, so they'll offer you a consignment option. The inventory is yours, but no one gets paid until the pieces sell. Generally, the split on consignment is 60/40, but that can vary. I've seen 50/50 to 80/20 splits. If there's room to negotiate work on making it a win/win that they can't resist.

Pricing items for consignment is almost like pricing for wholesale. The only differences are that you're getting a slightly higher percentage per item but you're not getting paid up front.

When considering your split negotiation, think about the cost of possible damage to your pieces, loss of your pieces and shipping costs (if you need to ship to the store). Those costs should be added to your variable costs and reflected in the pricing per piece.

For this scenario I'm not going to change our costs, but be aware of any extra charges you may have when doing consignment. I'm also giving you the high/low pricing because depending on the shop clientele, you may need to lower your pricing.

The pricing guideline suggestions are:

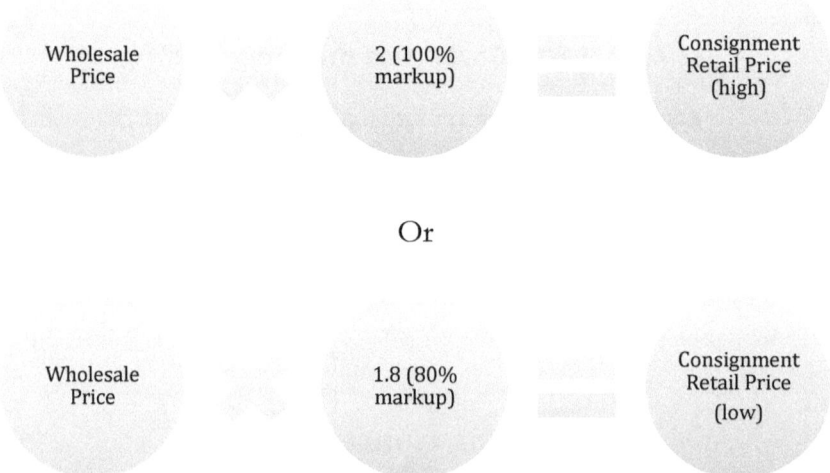

Or

Using our scarf scenario:

$59.15 x 2 = $118.30 consignment retail price high

$59.15 x 1.8 = $106.47 consignment retail price low

What this means for you at each split is:

- 50/50 split - $59.15 (high), $53.24 (low) for you as seller
- 60/40 split - $70.98 (high), $63.88 (low) for you as seller
- 70/30 split - $82.81 (high), $74.52 (low) for you as seller
- 80/20 split - $94.64 (high), $85.17 (low) for you as seller

Keeping the wholesale price and working with it for your consignment scale will be good for keeping your profit margin.

Commissioned Pieces

Commissioned pieces, especially from friends or family members, are usually the ones we lose the most money on when selling. I know because I too tend to over-discount the price because I feel bad charging my friends. Which is why I've trained myself to understand that my crochet is not a hobby but a business, I've also trained myself to get paid fairly, no matter what, for my business.

Now, before you start throwing stones and stop reading, I want to be the first to also say, you can do that while still offering your friends and family discounts. I will elaborate on that later in the book, so keep an eye out for that information.

Getting back to commissioned pieces, those are the projects that come along because someone (beyond family & friends) has seen what you can do and says "how much would it cost to do XYZ?" or "I'd like you to make XYZ for me; what would that cost?" Yippee! Someone has not only seen your work but admired it to the point they trust that you can create their fantasy item. Now what?

Remember that production cost you calculated at the beginning of the book? That number has actually been the basis for all your pricing so far; there's no reason why now would be any different.

Often, commissioned pieces are derivatives of items you've already made. A customer would like a familiar piece in a slightly different style or size, so they ask for a custom made piece; that is your commissioned piece. Pricing those pieces should be easy because you'll take the price

21

you have for the similar item and apply it to the commissioned item. If you're being asked to make something completely different from what you have in your inventory, you'll need to come up with some new pricing fast so you can get the sale and complete the agreement.

This is where I say start at the production cost and work your way back up to a fair retail price. I know what you're thinking: "but I don't know the production cost because this is the first time I'm making this item!" Well, technically that's true, but you can come up with a number if you consider what you already know about your business and how much it will cost to create the items you do have. Let's use an example.

You're at a craft fair selling scarves, hats, gloves, and some neck warmers. A customer comes to your booth and looks around. She tries on a few hats and gloves and decides to purchase a matching set.

As she's paying she asks, "Do you take custom orders?" You excitedly say, "Yes, of course!" Pleased to know that, she responds, "Great! Because I was thinking this set would look great with a poncho, but I just can't seem to find one that I would like anywhere. Would you be able to make a poncho to match this set? How much would that cost?"

You're suddenly nervous because you didn't expect her request to be so much larger than the items you currently have on hand. You know you can make a poncho, so you respond, "Yes, I would love to make a poncho to match this set. Give me a minute and I'll let you know what the price will be."

That's when you go to the back, pull out your calculator, and start punching numbers. What numbers? The ones I'm about to give you.

1. You already know a few things that will help you figure out the final cost of the commissioned piece within a few cents of a fair price. Using our scarf scenario, let's look at what they are: The largest piece you currently have displayed is the scarf
2. You know what the production cost for the scarf is
3. You know it will take about 3 times the resources to make the poncho than it did to make the scarf

Great! Now all you have to do is calculate the numbers and you'll have a price for your patron. Your formulas will look like this:

Our scarf scenario will look like this:

$45.50 x 3 = $136.50

Once you have that number, you do the wholesale price calculation:

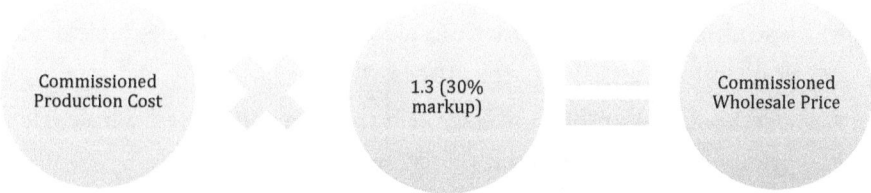

Our scarf scenario would look like this:

$136.50 x 1.3 = $177.45

That is now your wholesale price, not your retail price. We need to do one more calculation to get to the retail price you will give to your patron. That calculation will be:

Or

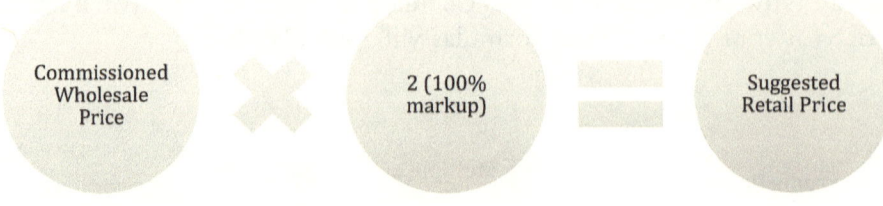

Our scarf scenario will look like this:

$$\$177.45 \times 1.8 = \$319.41$$

$$\$177.45 \times 2 = \$354.90$$

If, when you're done doing your calculations, you feel your numbers are too high, you have options because you are a little blind which allows for more flexibility. Here are a few things you could do:

- Use the commissioned wholesale price as your price; technically you do have a 30% margin there
- Use less than an 80% markup on the commissioned wholesale price; there is a whole range to choose from

Remember, all your pricing can be fluid up to a 100% markup, so it's up to you to figure out what works for your business and what you offer to your audience.

In a commission situation, use the numbers you already have as a basis for finding the numbers you need to come up with. I emphasize the wholesale price because once you go below your wholesale price, you're no longer in business, but in hobby mode, and won't be able to sustain for very long.

Commissioned pieces can be a great way to expand your skills and offerings. Once you've made one item, you'll find it easier to make more of the same.

Keep in mind the fact that it's easier to reduce your prices than it is to increase them.

Pricing for Friends & Family

Remember when I told you I'd talk about friends and family pricing? Well here we are. For me and for many others I've seen, pricing for friends and family is such a sensitive subject. For some reason we feel that we can't charge them; they're our friends, or that's my mom, aunt, cousin etc. The truth is the people closest to us are the ones to truly help support us.

When we charge them for our handmade pieces, we aren't doing something to them, we are continuing to build our businesses. That being said, we can offer them incentive simply because it's the nice thing to do, but let's make sure we aren't doing it and destroying our business in the process.

Here are a few ways I've discovered that work well when pricing for friends and family:

Offer them a price that is 30% off the 80% markup retail price

Offer them a price that is 50% off the 100% markup retail price

In our scarf scenario it looks like this:

$$\$106.47 - 30\% = \$74.53$$

$$\$118.30 - 50\% = \$59.15$$

Friends and family want to help us grow our businesses. They'll appreciate a discount and also understand why we need to give them a price at all. The more you think of your craft as a business, the more you'll realize the fairness in keeping to your pricing chart.

Non-Profit Pricing / Charitable Giving

The last section in this chapter is on non-profit pricing and charitable giving. There may be an opportunity for you to sell to a non-profit organization. Although it's nice to do, you don't need to have special pricing for non-profits.

Non-profits are usually able to pay what the market will bear, and they usually have money set aside for whatever they are proposing to do. If they want to carry your items in a shop, it's completely fair to charge them the same wholesale rate as you would any other retailer; having said that, it may be an opportunity for you to do something good for your community that can be written off on your taxes at the end of the year.

Giving your pieces away for charity is a nice way to spread the word about your business. What you want to make sure you do is keep a record of what you give and its retail value for tax filing purposes.

Charitable giving is also a way to reduce your tax liability at the end of the year. Keep good records and you should be fine. Also keep track of the items you give away for contests because those are marketing expenses that can also be accounted for on your taxes.

Chapter 3
Selling Patterns

Pricing and selling patterns is slightly different than selling completed pieces on the market for a few reasons; First, depending on the complexity of the pattern, they can take some time to develop; Second, because you're offering a tool, the pricing is lower because the expenses are lower than a completed piece; Third, payment for a pattern comes many times over, so lower pricing will give you an opportunity to get back the time value from creating the pattern many times over.

Depending on the site you're searching, patterns range in price from **Free to $10**. If we use the formula from the beginning of the book, we should be able to come up with pricing that will work to cover your costs (yes you still have business costs) and offer you a profit. Some things you definitely want to consider when pricing your patterns:

- Complexity of the pattern; the more complex, the more expensive
- The time you put into creating the pattern
- Payments you've made to make sure the pattern is readable
- Resources you've used to test the pattern
- Where you're selling
- Who you're selling to
- Profit needed on each pattern sale

Setting up a scale for yourself will make it easier to price your patterns vs. winging it every time you create a new pattern. If you have easy patterns that didn't take long to develop, you may want to consider offering them for free as incentives for customers to get a feel for your patterns or to sign up for your newsletter, etc. It also gives you the opportunity to engage them so they'll come again when looking for a new pattern.

When selling patterns, you still have quite a few fixed and variable costs to consider; depending on the pattern they aren't as high as on a completed piece. If you're the scarf seller, your fixed costs are still the same because you are still running your crochet business. The variable costs may be lower depending on how complex the pattern is. Just like we did for the completed scarf, let's figure out the wholesale cost for your patterns.

Calculate Total Fixed Costs for the month – These are the expenses incurred on a regular basis every month. They don't change no matter how many patterns you sell. (e.g. Website, rent, monthly subscription fees, monthly service fees, monthly marketing budget, etc.)

Calculate Total Variable Costs for the month – These are the expenses directly related to the development of your patterns. (e.g. listing or selling fees per pattern, number of hours to produce each pattern, incentives for pattern testing, payment for technical writing etc.)

Your Cost Per Pattern will then be calculated like this:

Keep in mind this is not your retail price, this number is just what it will cost you to create 2 patterns per month. So, if we want to work in hypothetical numbers, the calculation will be:

($83 + $82 / 2 patterns = $82.50 per pattern)

Now, I don't know anyone in their right mind who would purchase a crochet pattern for $82.50, so of course this number is not feasible. But, if you remove your time from the variable costs and use only the listing / selling fees associated with the patterns, you'll start seeing clearer.

($83 + $.4 / 2 patterns = $41.70 per pattern)

Another thing to consider: this is the number of patterns you've been able to create for the month, not the number of patterns you plan to sell. So, what if we used the number of patterns you project selling within the month then create a formula that looks like this:

Your formula is:

($83 + $.4 / 16 = $5.21 per pattern)

That is a more reasonable number, giving you the opportunity to sell 4 patterns per week. Now the question is what if you don't sell the 16 patterns that month? What then? Maybe the projected sales can be absorbed by another of your offerings (you sell more scarves than expected) or roll the number to the following month.

There are different ways to absorb the pricing because it's a lower price point. Also, you'll be adjusting your pattern pricing according to difficulty, so some patterns will be a little less than this base cost, and others will he higher. That will help cover the costs for the unsold patterns.

One more thing: you can choose to use the base price of $5.21, which is the "Production Cost" number, as your pricing starting point, or you can build in your 30% cushion and use that as the basis number.

Your formula is:

$5.21 x 1.3 = $6.77 per pattern

Using the final number of $6.77 as your base price allows you to have a built-in cushion giving you the flexibility to sell your patterns beyond your own shop without losing any money. If you aren't sure what your scale should look like, here's an example you can use.

- Easy pattern – less than 1 hour to make – Free
- Easy pattern – 1 hr–2.5 hrs to make - $6.77 x .6 = $4.06 (40% markdown)

- Easy to Intermediate pattern – 2.5–4.5 hrs to make $6.77 x .7 = $4.74 (30% markdown)
- Intermediate pattern – 4.5–8 hrs to make - $6.77
- Intermediate to advanced pattern – 8+ hrs to make - $6.77 x 1.1 = $7.45 (10% markup)
- Advanced pattern – 8+ hrs to make = $6.77 x 1.2 = $8.12 (20% markup)
- Advanced to Expert – 8+ hrs to make = $6.77 x 1.3 = $8.80 (30% markup)

This is a sample, but it gives you an idea of how to price your patterns depending to difficulty. Alter this scale as needed because you know your target audience and what your market will bear. Having a scale makes it easier for you to figure out which patterns you'd like to put more time into designing and what their pricing will be once you're done.

Selling Patterns to Yarn Shops

Now that you've calculated base costs for selling your patterns, and you've created a scale, you're ready to offer patterns for wholesale and to Yarn Shops. The basic formula is simple; take whatever price you've come up with and divide by 2 for the yarn shop pricing. Examples are:

- Easy to Intermediate - $4.74/2 = $2.37
- Intermediate - $6.77/2 = $3.39
- Intermediate / Advanced - $7.45/2 = $3.73
- Advanced - $8.12/2 = $4.06
- Advanced / Expert - $4.40

Yarn shop owners need a good cushion so you may also give them the suggested retail price of the patterns once you sell them at the agreed price. Showing them what type of cushion they have may entice them to purchase more patterns from you later.

The pricing used for the patterns will be the pricing used when selling your patterns wholesale.

Chapter 4
Getting Patterns Published

If you design and write your own patterns, you've wondered about getting published in the most popular crochet magazines. As far as pricing goes, until you are well known the magazines have their rates, and you either accept them or not. Period.

The exposure of having a pattern published in a national magazine is probably well worth the effort. Once you've been published, you can use that tear sheet and the experience in your biography. It gives you credibility, and who couldn't use that?

The first thing to do is look at a few copies of the magazine you're interested in getting published in to get an idea of the types of items they're looking for. Once you feel you've got a good handle on their market, find out who you need to contact. All the information you need is available on the magazine websites under "submissions." The person you contact will send you a submission calendar outlining the upcoming deadline(s) and what they are looking to publish in the upcoming issue(s). Follow directions then wait. It may take a few weeks before you hear back, so be patient. Also, do not submit the same pattern to two different publications; you may shoot yourself in the foot. It's okay to submit to several publications at the same time, just submit different patterns or articles to each. This bit of advice comes from direct experience of my first magazine submission. Thankfully, everyone understood and things went well.

eBooks (Self-Publishing)

Another good way to get published is to do it yourself. In this technologically advanced age, more people are choosing to get their content out by self-publishing. If you have several patterns you want to group together to create a booklet or eBook, then do the research and self-publish. If you have an informational book to publish, go for it.

When pricing a self-published book, consider the value you are delivering with your content. If it's a compilation of patterns, then consider the pricing you placed on the patterns and figure your price. If, it's an informational book that brings added value to your customer/client, then price according to what you think it's worth and make sure you're marketing makes the value clear.

When it comes down to it, most people buy based on value and not price, so deliver value in your eBook and price accordingly.

I know you're probably annoyed that I haven't given you a specific formula here. It can be a little frustrating, but since you now know your cost of production and/or delivery, it should be simple to add to your base price.

What I'm working on doing is not making you totally dependent on a formula, but to think about the value you're delivering to your audience and how much you think that value is worth. Self-publishing is the best place to start working on that because it's self-guided from the start.

Getting Published

What if you want to publish, but self-publishing is not for you? You're not really interested in doing all the work surrounding the marketing of your book yourself. That's fair. There are publishing houses that do publish craft books. Do your research and submit a query where possible. The pricing of the book won't be up to you, but being published comes with its own set of bragging rights that will help lift your trail to success.

My advice is to have a very good idea of what you're proposing and to make it as clear as possible to the publisher. It's also a good idea to see if you can get an agent to represent you once your book is accepted and especially if this is the first in a long line of books. Be prepared to do what is needed quickly or to wait for an answer. Know what you want and go for it. Don't forget to get a lawyer to help with the process.

Article Writing

Another way to get your information shared is to write articles for online blogs or magazines. If you submit your article to a database like "Ezine Articles," newsletters pertaining to crochet may pick it up giving you much wider exposure. Usually you won't get paid for these articles, but the exposure is a way to drive traffic to your website. Another venue online is Squidoo. You can create several lenses on any subject you choose then share them with your audience. They may also be picked up by others to be used in online publications so the time and effort is well worth it. Whatever you write will position you as an expert in the field and help when you're expanding into other areas.

Chapter 5
Teaching Crochet

You've learned to crochet, you've been doing it for some time, and you love it. One day a friend, co-worker, or stranger in the yarn section of a store asks you to teach them how to crochet. They're willing to pay you and they want to know how much it would cost to have a course from you. What do you say?

Well, I bet you say, "oh, you don't have to pay me, I'll do it for free." How do I know that's what you'll say? I've been there. I'm not going to go through all the reasons that would be the answer because I'm sure it jumped into your head as soon as I mentioned there were reasons. Instead, let's focus on why you will request a fee and how much you'll be asking.

You're an artisan. You are not a hobbyist; you're using your crochet skills to support your family. It's your craft. It's what you do, and it's a skill that you have that holds value on the open market. Those are only some of the reasons you'll ask for a fee to teach someone how to do your craft. If you have any questions about that, please read the first sentence again until you understand that being an artisan and making money from your art is noble and acceptable.

Now, I'm not going to lead you to believe that if your daughter came to you and wanted to learn to crochet you'd need to turn her away because you know she has no money. But what I want you to understand is this: It's okay to charge for your skill; please be fair (to your client and to yourself) and professional when in business.

Now that we know why we'll ask for a fee to teach, we need to know what we'll ask as a fee. The scale on teaching fees varies. What will your fees be? I bet you know what I'm going to say, but I'm going to say it anyway: "who your audience is, and the value delivered in your course, will determine your fees." You also want to consider your venue. Are you teaching online where the student may have continued access to the course even after the live course? Are you teaching in your living room where the student has direct access to you and your expertise? Are you providing any materials for the course? Developing your course will help you figure out what your fair market value is as a crochet instructor.

Another thing, if you're a certified instructor that may help with your fees also. In my opinion, most students are not going to look for a certificate that says that someone else who knows how to crochet has watched you and certifies that you know how to crochet and teach crochet. They are more interested in the fact that you know how to crochet, they like you, and your fees are fair.

So, let's get into the nitty gritty of your pricing. Please remember these are guidelines to help with your brainstorming; they are not hard and fast rules. Consider your market, your skill level, and your comfort with teaching and price accordingly.

Teaching Online

With online webinars and teleseminars, you have lots of options when it comes to teaching a course online. Below are some of the ideas I can give you for fees.

- Fee Range: $10 - $40 per class
- Duration: 1 – 3 hours
- Benefits: Full fee retention, recording is available on-demand forever, patterns or instructional materials offer with recording, re-sellable product, online support is offered on an on-going basis

Careful consideration of what you'll be offering and the value they'll bring to your students is key in helping to set the final price for any course you're offering online.

Teaching in the Community

When I talk about teaching in your community I'm talking about local yarn stores, community centers, local colleges, churches, and other venues where hobby courses are taught. The fees for these courses have a smaller range, and the pricing may also depend on the venue's normal fees. It's your time, so you need to consider whether the fee offered is worth your time.

- Fee Range: $10 - $20 per class/per student
- Duration: 1 – 3 hours
- Benefits: Community involvement, local recognition, hands on teaching experience

When doing a class at a venue, there may be a percentage fee to be paid to the venue but exposure as an instructor is good and the fee is usually small.

Chapter 6
Public Speaking

This chapter is not for everyone. I know the number one fear of people is public speaking, so if this is not your cup of tea, read it anyway; you may find something interesting that you can use or pass along.

Those who would like to add public speaking engagements to the list of services they offer will benefit from their craft. The fees for public speaking vary more than any other range we've spoken about so far.

There's a reason for that: the venues and events you'll be asked to participate in will vary just as much. In the realm of public speaking there are no absolute numbers. There are levels that you can choose to follow, but even those vary depending on who you're asking. I put this section into this book because if you have an expertise and you can deliver the message or the know-how effectively, there is no reason why public speaking should not be part of your portfolio.

Just like we did in the beginning when we figured our costs per piece, we need to do the same when figuring out how much to ask as a speaker. There are some factors that will influence your fees, but the ones I think are most important are these:

- How much do you want to make? (hourly, daily etc.)
- How much will the market bear?
- How much is it going to cost you to attend the function? (are you paying or are they)
- How much prep time are you putting into the event?
- How long is the engagement? (60 minutes or 3 days)
- How much potential is there in the audience for client or customer conversion?
- Do you want to do the engagement?

Once you've done your research and come up with a scale that works for you, remember to stick with it. As a speaker who is just starting out, there may be times when you want to work for a minimal amount so you can perfect your message and delivery. Getting some teaching experience will help you get comfortable before an audience. Once you are more comfortable, just as I encouraged you to stick with your wholesale price, it's important to stick to your base speaking price. There will, of course, be times when you'll go below your base (remember the friends & family thing), but for the most part, unless there's a very compelling reason to participate at a conference, I do not advise going below your range.

Unfortunately, I'm not going to give you a formula here. There are too many variables that are very specific to each situation. I want you to understand that underpricing yourself as a speaker is just as bad for your efforts as underpricing your completed pieces.

If you don't take your expertise seriously, why should anyone else? At the end of the book I will list some resources for extra information on speaking fees and how to set your price. If you're comfortable doing public appearances, it may be a very good source of income for you.

Some of the venues you may consider targeting for your public speaking expertise include:

- Conferences
- Local Yarn Shops
- Fairs
- Bookstores (If you've published a book)

But before approaching anyone, make sure you have your scale ready and that you're open to knowing and understanding what the market will bear.

Chapter 7
Pattern Testing

This is going to be a very brief chapter. The information I've received from various sources as well as my own experience says the thinking on how to pay pattern testers is varied. It seems to be a consensus in the industry that there is no real pay for pattern testing. There is a network in the various national organizations where pattern testers are paid, but it is a well-guarded secret. There are some knitting and crochet professionals who believe in not only getting paid as professionals but offering to pay their testers as best they can for the skills they bring to the project. As a pattern tester you are expected to do the following:

- Work up a usable sample of a pattern
- Flag and/or fix any technical issues you encounter on a pattern
- Consult with the designer on what you discovered while working up the pattern
- Retain confidentiality of the project until its official release

Below are some of the ways pattern testers are compensated for the part they play in helping get a complete and error-free pattern to the market:

- Free copy of the completed pattern
- Materials used to complete the pattern
- Sometimes payment per yard (up to $.20 per yard)

When agreeing to be a pattern tester it's important to consider your time and how testing works into your business plans. If you believe working as a tester will forward your goals, then go for it. Remember, just like everything else, it needs to work for you and your business.

Conclusion

Crochet is fun and can be rewarding financially if you have a plan for your business. Take the time to figure out what your expenses are, what type of items you like to make, and where you want to sell. Learn about your target market and what they are looking for, and then deliver with confidence, knowing you are fairly priced for great sales.

Remember, everything you've just read are guidelines to get you pointed in the right direction. If you need more help, enlist the services of a financial professional to help you make the best decision possible in your crochet business.

It is my sincere hope that in reading this guide you've gotten a clearer picture of what it means to be in business for yourself. Pricing your expertise takes preparation, and determination. Knowing that you're fairly pricing your items or expertise allows you to move forward with confidence with the business of presenting your pieces to your audience because you took the time to know who they are.

Go forth and conquer with a spirit of fairness, humility and service and you will not fail. I wish you more success than you dream because big dreams are what move mountains.

Resources

Public Speaking additional information

Books:

- **The Complete Guide to Public Speaking by Jeff Davidson** - *This book offers bold insight into what it takes to succeed as a public speaker. Six major topic areas include identifying and developing a dynamite speaking topic; enlivening your presentations with humor, movement, and stories; positioning and marketing your speech; winning and negotiating speaker contracts; building groundwork activities leading up to the performance; and inspiring audiences.*

- **Speak for a Living by Anne Bruce** - *Speak for a Living shows readers how to take their natural talents to the next level by becoming an in demand speaker and trainer at venues around the world. Readers will learn how to get into the speaking business; how to get consistent bookings, and what marketing tools are necessary to make it all happen.*

- **Million Dollar Speaking by Alan Weiss** - *Alan Weiss offers the inside advice you need to turn your talent into a high-paying career—from honing your delivery skills to building a business.*

Websites:

- How to Set your speaking fee - *http://www.psychotactics.com/blog/speaking-fee/*

- How to calculate your Speaking Fees - *http://www.startawildfire.com/free-resources/articles-and-hot-tips/how-to-determine-your-speaking-fees*

- The Ultimate Guide to Keynote Speaker Fees - *http://evanbailyn.com/keynotespeakers/the-ultimate-guide-to-keynote-speaker-fees/*

Article Publishing Websites:

- http://www.squidoo.com
- http://www.ehow.com
- http://ezinearticles.com
- http://www.hubpages.com
- http://www.examiner.com

Other Business Building Resources

- 5 Steps to Successfully Starting a Crochet Business
- Yarn Obsession, Crochet for Financial Freedom
- Hooking for Cash, The Crochet Business Blog
- Crocheting for Profit

Bonus Section:
How to Find Your Target Market

Chapter 1
Why do I need to know my target market?

"Is it really important to know my target market?" Well, let me put it this way, is it important for your pilot to know his destination? Is it important for a fisherman to know where there are likely to be more fish? Yes, it is! Just like the pilot and the fisherman, you need to know where you're going and how to get there. So, the first thing you need to know is who's going to take you there.

Studying your audience isn't hard. What you're trying to do is connect the right person, your audience, to the right item, your product. If you're selling high end watches to middle-income teens, you're probably not going to stay in business for very long because the percentage of teens who can afford high-end watches will be relatively small. But, if you were to target wealthy teens the odds would certainly be in your favor.

So, why would you need to know your target market? Here are a few reasons:

- You'll know where to find them
- You'll know what they want and deliver it
- You'll know what to charge
- You'll know why they want what you have to offer
- You'll know what attracts them
- You'll know where to look for them

Knowing your target audience gives you the freedom to market to the exact audience you want to reach without wasting marketing dollars. Simply brilliant!

The makers of a product or service will usually sit down at the beginning of development to decide who their audience is. Deciding the audience gives them a blueprint of how to move forward with their strategy. It's the same for small business owners, we need to think about who we want to reach then go find them where we know they are.

There are products and services we can all benefit from and yet companies spend millions of dollars targeting particular market segments. The next time you see a commercial, think about who they are speaking to, it is you? Orange juice, beer, soda etc. they are all targeted to particular audiences. Your product or service should be too.

Chapter 2
Know your product

Before you can begin the journey toward finding your target audience or market you have to know your product / service so well the rest becomes intuitive. Close self-examination will give you the information you need to go out and find the match for your product / service. Here are a few things you'll need to think about when working through your self-examination.

Purpose

What is the purpose of your product or service? Does it satisfy a basic need or is it is a luxury item? Is your item for a niche audience, or is the audience broader? Knowing the purpose of your items will give you an immediate audience in mind. This is where we stop with our target market efforts because we think the broad category we're thinking of is enough for us to target our market. Every market can and should be made smaller.

Uniqueness

What makes your product/service unique in the marketplace? Are there others selling the same item? If so, what makes yours stand out? If not how can you show the value? What is your unique selling proposition? The hard part these days is that having great service isn't really enough because people have to experience your service by doing business with you. There needs to be an angle that can be easily seen through your branding (we'll talk about that in the next booklet of this series) and marketing efforts.

Customers

Who are your current customers? What do they buy from you? Why do they buy those items from you? What do they have in common? How much do they spend? Do they come back or are most of your customer's first-time buyers? Do surveys of your current customer base to find out the answers to these questions. If you have a product / service that relies on repeat customers, but your customer base is made up of 'one-time' client/customers, you need to know that and adjust as needed.

Benefits

Why would anyone want to buy your product or service? Does it satisfy a need or a want? Is it a solution to a problem your audience has? Can it improve your customer's life in some way? If so, are you effectively teaching that information?

Knowing the answers to these questions for yourself gives you a foundation to start looking for the perfect target market for your product/service. Without knowing these answers you won't know what to look for in an audience or how to talk to that audience once you've figured out who they are.

Chapter 3
What is your demographic profile?

Let's start with the basics of how to find your target market. The first thing to look at is the demographic profile of the audience you'd like to reach. What's that? Well, it's the basics of who they are. Age, gender, income, location and marital status are all pieces of information that help shape your marketing story to fit your audience.

Age

How old is the audience you want to target? Are they teens? Seniors? Middle-age? Every stage of life comes with a different set of needs, desires, responsibilities and income. When you decide the age of your target market you're closer to maximizing your marketing dollars.

Gender

The gender of your target market will tell you a lot about their needs. Men and women work, think and shop in very different ways. If your product or service is targeted to men, you'll need different information than if your product is targeted to women. You also have different things to think about if your products are targeted to women for men or to men for women. Knowing your audience is majority men or women will help you know what to do and where you reach them.

Income

As I mentioned before, if you're product is high-end watches and your marketing is reaching middle income teens, you won't be in business very long. What you're delivering and the income bracket you're delivering too makes a difference in your marketing efforts. If it takes $50 per item for delivery you'll need to decide which income level you need to target with your marketing so you can sell at the price needed to keep your business growing.

Education

The level of education your audience has does play a part in how they will view their shopping and your product / service. Knowing this information will help you decide your business voice and language. Whether your language is formal or very informal can be influenced by the level of education your audience has and how you need to reach them.

Location

Where can you find your audience? Are your products / services local, regional, national or international? What do you need to know about your audience's location that will help in your marketing efforts? Your audience's location is vital to how you'll reach them and the message you'll use. Consider location carefully, especially if you're international and dealing with cultures that aren't your own. The wrong message will kill your business quickly if it's not delivered in a sensitive and respectful manner.

Marital / Family Status

Believe it or not, the marital / family status of your audience matters. Married, single, divorced, or widowed your audience has a different perspective depending on the category they fall into. Knowing their status will allow you to speak directly to their immediate needs and offer solutions to help.

Now that you've thought about the surface demographics of your target market, you're ready to go a little deeper and start thinking about their Psychographics. That only means you'll now be looking at how your audience thinks, feels and acts, fleshing them out into a two-dimensional figure rather than a flat portrait.

Chapter 4
Values and Lifestyle

Once you've gotten through the demographics, it's time to dig deeper and figure out what their psychographics are. Figure out their values and lifestyle so you know where to find them and how to speak to them.

Most Valuable

What is most valuable to your audience? Depending on what you've learned by their demographics, what do you think is most valuable to them in their lives right now? Is it security? Luxury? Health? Money? Whatever they value most is important to help you create a message that speaks directly to their needs.

Information Sources

Where does your audience get their decision-making information? Are they television watchers or newspaper and magazine readers? Do they research the internet or read books? Knowing where they're looking to make a purchase decision will help you know where to place yourself to be found. You'll also know which blogs, magazines or newspapers would maximize any interviews or promotions you're doing to reach your audience with your product /service.

First Responders / Followers

Something you may not know plays a part in how you interact with your target market is how they respond to the marketplace. First responders are those who jump on as soon as something new hits the market because they want the newest thing. They also want to be the first to have the new thing to show their friends and peers. Followers take their time to find out if something is what they want or need. They research and will jump in on the second or third iteration of an item. Knowing this about your audience will help you with timing and audience segmentation when it comes to your marketing.

Chapter 5
Product Interaction

The next step is knowing how your audience will use your product / service. Without knowing that your marketing is going to fall on deaf ears because you won't be talking to the right wants or needs.

Benefits

Is what you're offering something valuable to them? If so how? What will your offering do to make their lives better? Think of your buying habits. When you go to buy something aren't you buying for a benefit? What's the feeling your customer will get or the need that will be taken care of by buying what you're offering? Answer these questions for a clear idea of how to present your offerings to the marketplace.

Customer Survey

A great way to find out what benefits your customers are getting is asking current customers about their experience with your offerings. What do they like or dislike about what you offer? Are they using your offerings in ways you've never thought of? You'll be able to find out more about your offerings and your customers by doing simple surveys and tracking the results.

Need vs. Want

Does what you offer help fill a basic need or does it increase the quality of life but isn't entirely necessary? Talking to needs & wants are different. If you're a luxury item seller then you want to sell a lifestyle or fantasy. If you're a seller of basic needs, the benefits are most important because you'll need to stand out in a more saturated market. Making what you offer stand out means you've found an angle or a story that appeals to your audience and helps them do business with you.

Knowing how your audience interacts with your product or why they use your service is vital to the branding of your business.

Chapter 6
Creating a Profile

Once you've gathered all the information from the previous chapters you now want to create a prototype person. That prototype person will represent your target market, the audience you want to talk too directly.

Start by giving them a name, an age, and a job.

Once you've gotten those basic things figured out, give them a life.

- Does he/she have a family? If so, how many children do they have?
- Where do they live?
- What are their interests?
- How much education do they have?
- What keeps them up at night?

Finally, write out their attributes so that when you're creating your advertising and marketing campaigns you keep this prototype person you've created in mind. You'll get to know them well because you'll be creating them as you gather information and learn more about them.

Finding your target market is almost like developing a character in a book or play based on people and circumstances relevant to your product / service. Have fun! Getting to know your target market is a great way to get to know your customers and potential customers better. It's also the best way to serve them well.

Chapter 7
Conclusion

Don't let finding your target market be the thing to hold you back in business. Learning about and getting to know your audience should be a fun enlightening process. Knowing you'll maximize your marketing dollars by being laser targeted should help with your decision.

If you find the process scary, do one step at a time. You can break it up into days or weeks or months, but do the work and get the information. You'll be happy you did.

www.ingramcontent.com/pod-product-compliance
Lightning Source LLC
Chambersburg PA
CBHW021928170526
45157CB00005B/2233